How to Bluff Your Way into Space

Paul Mason
Illustrated by Klaus Meinhardt

Contents

OXFORD
UNIVERSITY PRESS

Bluff your way into space

Training to be an astronaut is REALLY hard. You have to be super-clever. You also have to be super-fit, a good team member but also able to work alone. On top of that, you have to undergo YEARS of training. Most astronauts don't make it into space before they're 40 years old!

If all that sounds a bit tricky and time-consuming, don't panic – just bluff your way into space instead. All you really need is THIS BOOK. It's jam-packed with information about the spacecraft, spacewalks, space food – all you need to become an expert in no time!

Top tips for space bluffers

Of course, bluffing your way into space without any proper training isn't easy – so this book is filled with top tips to make sure you rocket ahead!

A SPACE HERO SPEAKS

"Exploration is wired into our brains. If we can see the horizon, we want to know what's beyond."
Astronaut Buzz Aldrin explains why people want to explore space (even those who can't be bothered to do the training!).

Get set for lift-off on page 10.

Find out why these astronauts have gone for a dip. Turn to page 7.

BLAST FROM THE PAST

Panels like this one will tell you about key moments in the exploration of space. Learn from the past and maybe your future will lie in the stars.

A SPACE HERO SPEAKS

This is where you'll get inside info on what some top space explorers think, like Buzz Aldrin. Dropping their names into conversation will help you fit in with the real astronauts.

SECRET LINGO

Using insider 'lingo' (words that ordinary people don't know), is the best way to make yourself sound like an expert on any subject. For example, a 'Moon buggy' is called a 'Lunar Roving Vehicle' – or even better, an 'LRV'.

SPACED OUT!

Want to learn all kinds of fascinating and quirky facts about space? This is the place to look. If you mention these while chatting to other space travellers, you'll have them fooled.

Get ready to walk amongst the stars. Turn to page 24!

This *is* rocket science

You know when someone says, "It's not rocket science!" because the thing they are describing is easy? Well, the info on this page *is* rocket science and it's *not* easy. Of course, no one is going to expect you to actually build a rocket – that's a specialist job. But astronauts ARE expected to know how their spacecraft work, in case something goes wrong.

The first thing you'll need to know is what to call your spacecraft. If you call it a 'space rocket', people will look at you oddly. The proper name is 'launch vehicle' or 'launcher'. The rocket is only a part of this, the part that flames come out of as the launch vehicle is pushed into space. (Also, remember that 'push' is called 'thrust' in proper space-science language.)

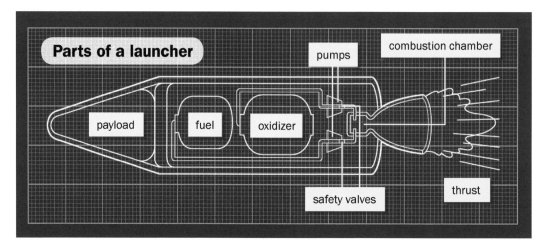

Parts of a launcher

payload | fuel | oxidizer | pumps | combustion chamber | safety valves | thrust

How much rocket power do you need?

The kind of rocket you need depends on the weight of the load it's carrying. A light **payload** only needs a relatively small amount of *thrust* to get into space – a launch vehicle with just one rocket is enough. A load of astronauts and science equipment needs more thrust, so the launch vehicle has extra rockets. These are **jettisoned** once they are empty of fuel to cut weight.

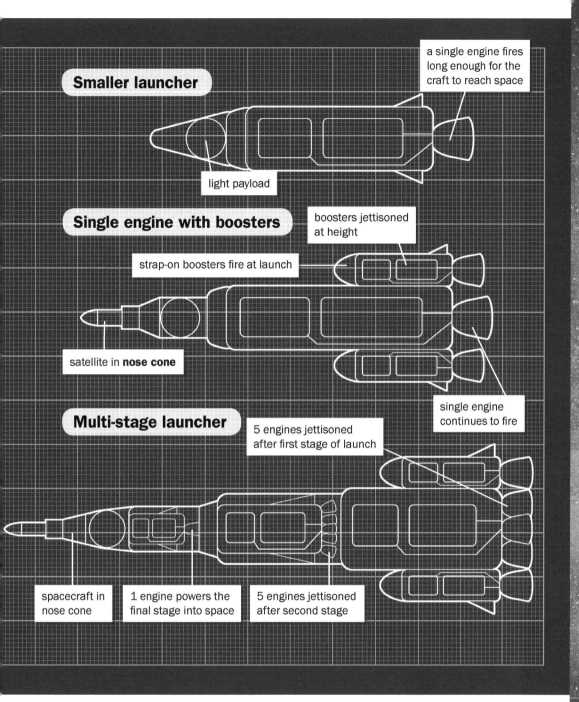

Smaller launcher

a single engine fires long enough for the craft to reach space

light payload

Single engine with boosters

boosters jettisoned at height

strap-on boosters fire at launch

satellite in **nose cone**

single engine continues to fire

Multi-stage launcher

5 engines jettisoned after first stage of launch

spacecraft in nose cone

1 engine powers the final stage into space

5 engines jettisoned after second stage

BLAST FROM THE PAST

The USA's *Saturn V* launch vehicles took astronauts to the Moon in the 1960s and 1970s. They were the biggest launch vehicles ever built: 110 metres tall and weighing 2799 tonnes.

Desperate to find out what to wear for lift-off? Turn to page 9!

Welcome to Zero-G

Zero-G might *sound* like a rap star but it's not. It's actually space slang for 'zero gravity'. Unless you understand what it is and prepare for it, you'll be sick with embarrassment. Actually, many astronauts do spend their first days in space throwing up! Unless you prepare for Zero-G, you'll probably be literally sick, too.

How can there be zero gravity?

DON'T ask that question among space **buffs** – they'll know you're a bluffer! Gravity is a force that pulls all objects towards each other. Big, **dense** objects have more gravity. Planet Earth is massive and relatively dense so it has a strong pull. That's why instead of floating off into space, we can walk around happily on its surface.

The further you are from an object, the weaker its gravitational pull. 100 kilometres and more above the Earth's surface, the planet's pull is so weak that it's not really there. Humans just float about, like jellyfish in the sea. That's Zero-G.

SPACED OUT!

The force of gravity feels different depending which planet you are on. Here are a couple of examples:

- Venus has only 90% of Earth's gravity, so you would feel lighter than usual.

- Neptune has 114% of Earth's gravity, so you would feel heavier and find it harder to move around.

Training for Zero-G

If you can get your body used to feeling weightless, it may stop you suffering from **space sickness** when you're floating around in space. There are three main ways to practise being in Zero-G:

1. On a special plane (known as the Vomit Comet!), which falls back to Earth at a speed that matches the force of gravity on Earth. The result is that everyone on board starts floating about.

2. Underwater in a deep-water pool, wearing a special diving suit.

3. Using POGO, which is a system of pulleys that makes a person almost weightless as they would be on the Moon.

▲ Zero-gravity on board the Vomit Comet.

▼ Astronauts train in a **centrifuge** to prepare for the G-force.

SPACED OUT!

Astronauts (including bluffers!) don't just have to cope with Zero-G. During lift-off, they also experience **4-G**. That's right – four times Earth's gravitational pull. Pressed into their seats, they can barely lift their arms. Without training, it would be difficult to operate the controls.

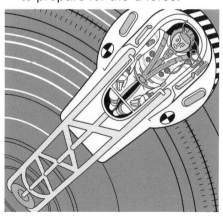

How to dress well

Being an astronaut is a bit like going to a fancy-dress party – if you don't wear the right clothes, you won't fit in. A **spacesuit** is a complicated thing: there are about 25 stages to putting it on. On Earth, the suit weighs twice as much as the astronaut inside it. In Zero-G, of course, it weighs nothing.

Your spacesuit is your friend

Your spacesuit will keep you alive in conditions where without it you'd be dead in nanoseconds. It supplies you with air to breathe: there's none in space. It protects you from extreme temperatures: in space, when the sun is shining on you, the temperature can reach 135°C, while in darkness, it can drop as low as -100°C.

There are different designs of suit for inside a craft, going on a spacewalk or walking around on the surface.

The need to pee

It takes 45 minutes to don a spacesuit. Pretty much the first thing you put on is a space nappy. You might not want to wee when you *start* donning your suit – but by the time you've reached the space station ten hours later, you almost certainly will.

SECRET LINGO

Putting on a spacesuit is called 'donning' it, and taking it off is called 'doffing' it. (If you get this wrong, people will realize you're a bluffer.)

◀ Astronaut Koichi Wakata gets help donning the training version of his suit.

Essential parts

1. **Snoopy** cap: microphone and headphones for voice communication

2. helmet

3. **retractable** visor cuts down **glare**

4. inner layers: about ten layers, including insulation to keep the body at a constant temperature

5. hard outer suit

6. inner and outer gloves

7. space nappy or 'maximum absorption garment', in case the astronaut needs a **comfort break**

8. in-suit drink bag

9. battery

10. life-support unit for oxygen, cooling, electricity and radio

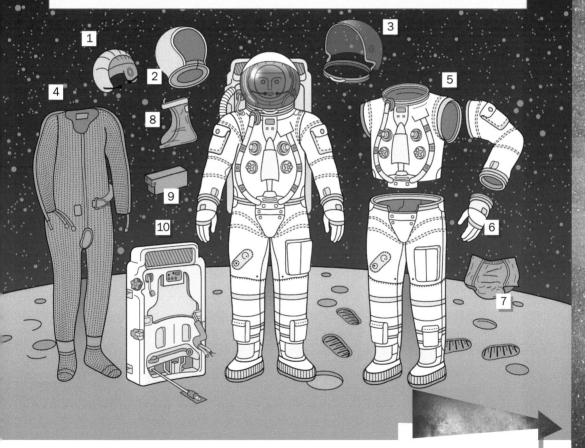

▲ The soft cap worn by astronauts is called a Snoopy cap because of the way the internal headphones hang down, like the dog's ears. Snoopy, a cartoon character, is also said to be a lucky mascot for US astronauts.

Want to find out how your spacesuit can help you make a spacewalk? Turn to page 25!

Preparing for lift-off

If there's one thing every astronaut really needs to know about, it's lift-off. Preparations for this start *weeks* before the launch vehicle actually takes off. However, you won't see much of the final week's activity because the whole crew will be in **quarantine!**

Quarantine time

About ten days before departure, all crew members have a detailed medical to check that no one is about to get sick. A week before departure, they are isolated in a clean, germ-free room to make sure they don't pick up any new bugs. If everyone became ill in space, it could affect the success of the mission, or even its safety.

◄ Astronauts are not just quarantined before take-off. The Apollo 11 crew spent three weeks in quarantine after their mission to walk on the Moon in 1969.

The closeout crew

About four hours before lift-off, you and the real astronauts start to put on your spacesuits. Then, at the launch pad, you meet up with the 'closeout crew'. These are experts who strap everyone into their seats, shut the spacecraft hatch and make all the final checks – before moving away to a safe distance.

Need a reminder about how your launch vehicle's rockets work? Turn to page 4!

LESSONS FROM THE PAST

Space travel is dangerous, particularly during lift-off. In 1967 fire broke out during a launch practice for the first Moon mission (Apollo 1). Three astronauts died. Two years of safety improvements followed, including the development of non-flammable materials, safer wiring and better emergency hatches.

▲ The Apollo 1 crew (Roger Chaffee, Edward White and Gus Grissom) training for the Apollo 1 mission. The three astronauts were killed during a launch pad testing session.

Countdown to lift-off

2–15 hours	Rocket and spacecraft systems powered up for checks
4 hours	Loading liquid oxygen begins
3.5 hours	Loading rocket fuel begins
3 hours	Fuelling complete (as late as possible for safety)
4 hours	Astronauts begin final preparations
3 hours	Astronauts enter spacecraft
2 hours	Astronauts are shut into craft

15 minutes	Team decides 'go or no-go'
10 minutes	Computer automatic countdown begins
5 minutes	Liquid oxygen loading complete
2 minutes	Final order to 'go'
1 minute	Engines ready to fire
10 seconds	Engines begin to build to full power
1 second	Bolts and brackets release rocket for lift-off
0	Lift-off!

No going back – it's lift-off!

You've been strapped into your seat in the launch vehicle, the closeout crew have sealed all the hatches and the final countdown has begun. Once the launch rockets have started firing and the vehicle starts to tremble with power, there really is NO WAY out.

Escape velocity

'3, 2, 1 … Lift-off.' The rockets fire, and the crew is pressed back into their seats. This is where the 4-G training comes in! During this part of the flight, the launch vehicle's rockets battle with gravity, which is trying to pull the vehicle back to Earth. (Gravity also pulls your face backward at this point, making you look like something out of a horror film.) Finally, the launch vehicle reaches a speed that allows it to break free of Earth's gravity – this is **escape velocity**.

▲ Astronaut Timothy Peake, from the UK, training in the Soyuz simulator in Star City, Russia, 2010.

A SPACE <u>HERO</u> SPEAKS

"When you launch in a rocket, you're not really flying that rocket. You're just sort of hanging on."
US astronaut Michael Anderson

SECRET LINGO

Don't refer to your travels into space as a 'visit' or a 'trip': this will immediately give you away as a bluffer. Its proper name is a 'mission'.

Into orbit

Once the spacecraft has begun to pull free of Earth's gravity, the mission commander uses bursts of rocket power to reach the right height for it to go into orbit. This is a point high above the Earth's surface, where gravity is balanced against the forces trying to push the craft still higher. Once there, the spacecraft stays at this height, circling the Earth.

▲ Most manned spacecraft go into **Low Earth Orbit** (LEO). The average height of this is 420 kilometres above the Earth's surface. The average speed is 7.7 kilometres per second.

◀ Back on Earth, the mission control room can see every detail of what's happening on board the spacecraft, via **telemetry.**

Staying in space

Your mission could be a simple space flight or it could be more complicated than this. It could take you to stay on a space station, high above the Earth. The non-bluffers in the crew will have been practising to live in space for at least a year and a half. They will have used a full-size training station, simulators and virtual-reality environments. You haven't done any of this, so here's a quick guide to space stations.

Getting on board the space station

It takes about six hours for a transfer vehicle to reach a space station in Low Earth Orbit. Once it has arrived, the transfer vehicle will **dock** with the space station. As soon as there is an airtight seal between the launch vehicle and the space station, one of the astronauts will open the connecting hatches, crawl through and climb on board their new space home.

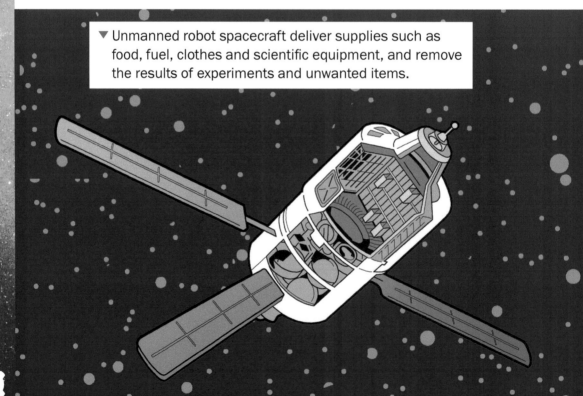

▼ Unmanned robot spacecraft deliver supplies such as food, fuel, clothes and scientific equipment, and remove the results of experiments and unwanted items.

1. docked supply craft
2. storage module
3. airlock for astronaut entry and exit
4. robot arm
5. research module
6. laboratory module
7. solar panels provide power
8. living module
9. main truss (girder)

SECRET LINGO

To reach the space station from their launch vehicle, astronauts use a craft sometimes called a 'transfer vehicle'. Calling it a 'space minibus' or similar will definitely show you to be a bluffer!

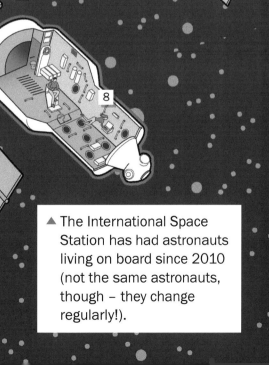

▲ The International Space Station has had astronauts living on board since 2010 (not the same astronauts, though – they change regularly!).

Space food

By the time you arrive at the space station, it will be more than ten hours since you started putting on your spacesuit. (Your space nappy might not be in very good shape by now!) Once you have changed into more-comfortable clothes, you'll be ready for a good meal. However, eating on board the space station may not be quite what you expected.

Having dinner in Zero-G

Can you imagine always having to eat your food out of a plastic bag? Well, that's what it's like eating in space. The reason is that at Zero-G, anything that isn't tied down will float about. Little bits of food – crumbs, for example – could clog up air vents, damage equipment, or drift into people's eyes, nose or ears. So things like salt and pepper are only available in liquid form, for squirting on to your food. ANYTHING that might float away has to be kept in its container.

Cosmic cooking

If you think cooking on Earth is complicated, you'll probably think again after trying out this space recipe.

Space pasta

Ingredients
- Onion
- Garlic
- Sun-dried tomatoes
- Olive oil
- Pasta

1. Slice the onion and garlic and put them in a foil wrapper. Add some olive oil, close the wrapper and turn on the food heater.

2. Repeat with the sun-dried tomatoes but use water instead of olive oil. If there's any tuna in the cupboard, you can add that too.

3. Add water to some pre-packed spaghetti and put it in another food heater.

4. Empty all three wrappers into one big food bag, shake it up and start eating.

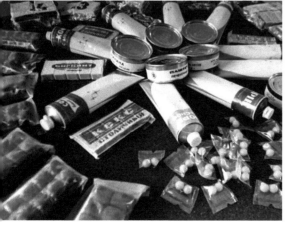

BLAST FROM THE PAST

Eating in space may be challenging nowadays but the food has got a lot better since the early days of space exploration. Back then, astronauts complained that the food, which was usually contained in a giant toothpaste tube, was tasteless and difficult to eat.

◀ A selection of the food taken on board space flights by Russian cosmonauts in the 1960s.

The space toilet challenge

Eating and drinking on the space station have unavoidable results – namely, poo and wee. In Zero-G you can't deal with these in the same way as you do on Earth. Special measures are needed! If you're going to successfully bluff your way through space, you'd better know about them!

Space toilets

In the early days of space travel, astronauts used to collect their poo in a refuse bag. This was wrapped up, and taken back to Earth. Who says being an astronaut isn't glamorous?

On a modern space station, the toilet looks a bit like the one back home. You have to strap yourself into it, though, to avoid floating off. Unlike toilets at home, there's no water, so fans suck the waste away instead.

A SPACE **HERO** SPEAKS

"There is some suction – but I must admit, you have to have a pretty good aim." *Former ISS commander Suni Williams describes the challenges of weeing in space.*

Want a reminder of the effects of Zero-G? Turn back to page 6!

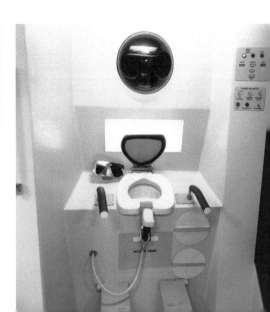

▶ A zero-gravity toilet designed by NASA for use on the US Space Station Freedom.

Waste away

Where does all that waste go? Well, poo is stored before being taken away on a robot supply ship. Wee is collected and recycled, along with every other drop of wastewater on board – even water vapour from breath and sweat. Once purified, the wastewater is added back into the general water supply – including the drinking water!

A SPACE HERO SPEAKS

"The water that we generate is much cleaner than anything you'll ever get out of any tap in the United States."
Layne Carter, Marshall Space Flight Center, describes the purity of the recycled water on a space station.

Bathroom basics

There's no bathroom in space, just your 'personal hygiene kit' stuck to the wall. When you clean your teeth, don't look around for a basin to spit into because there isn't one. Instead, you spit into a flannel. You wash your hair and body without water, using special shampoos and soaps.

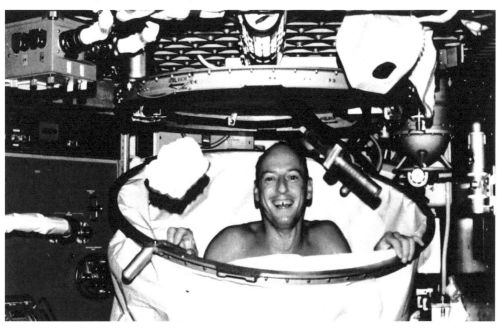

▲ The early Skylab space station had a shower with water – but it leaked!

How do you sleep when there's no up or down?

After a hard day's space travel, you'll be ready for a good night's sleep. Unfortunately, this presents a few problems in space. For a start, there's no proper bedtime: in orbit, the sun rises every 90 minutes. 'Night' lasts for 45 minutes. If you're going to bluff successfully, you need to know what to expect and remember – don't look surprised!

Which room is mine?

You *might* get a room, sort of, if the space station isn't too busy. The 'rooms' are actually little cupboards. In Zero-G, you can't just lie down because you would float away: a tight space is best for sleeping. At least the rooms/cupboards are soundproofed: you can listen to music or watch a DVD, which might take your mind off your bedroom's similarity to a shoebox.

A SPACE HERO SPEAKS

"You get to one side, you bounce off one wall and head in the opposite direction."

Astronaut Steve Smith describes what it's like trying to sleep in Zero-G when you're not tied down.

▶ Bunk beds on board the Space Shuttle *Endeavour* in 1994.

Looking for a reminder of how real astronauts train for space-station living? Turn to page 14!

No space!

Of course, if the space station is *busy*, you might not even get a room. (You're much less likely to get one if you aren't staying for long.) Instead, you'll have to sleep in a sleeping bag strapped to the wall. Use an eye mask to block out the light and some earplugs to shut out the noise, and try to get some **shut-eye**.

SPACE LINGO

A bedroom on a space station isn't called a 'room' (or even a 'cupboard'). Remember to refer to it as a 'TSS', which stands for Temporary Sleep Station, and you'll fit right in.

▶ ESA astronaut Paolo Nespoli in his sleeping bag in the Node-2 module of the International Space Station. Also known as Harmony, the module was delivered to the International Space Station in 2007.

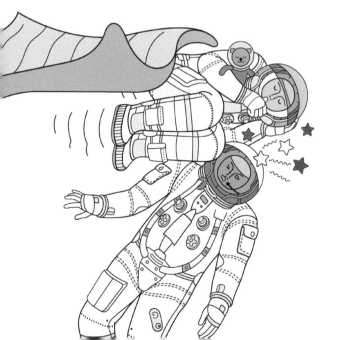

SPACED OUT!

On a space station, astronauts are woken by an alarm clock. On other spacecraft, however, they are usually woken by music, piped to them from Mission Control back on Earth. Sometimes the music is their choice, sometimes it's picked by Mission Control or by a family member back home.

Welcome to the space zoo

While you're up in space, expect to be experimented on. **DON'T PANIC!** All members of the crew are constantly monitored to see how living in space is affecting them. They're not the only ones. There could be ants, butterflies, crickets, flies, worms, snails, spiders, frogs, fish, mice ... even a small bird called a quail on the space station with you!

Bathroom basics

There is a long history of animals in space – in fact, they were there before humans. In the early days, no one was sure whether living creatures could survive the forces involved in space travel so experimental missions using animals instead of humans were launched to see what happened.

These days, animals are taken into space mainly to investigate the effects of Zero-G. They are also used for other biological and medical experiments, such as recovery from exposure to **radiation**.

▲ Laika is the most famous space animal ever. She was even pictured on a stamp! She was sent into orbit in 1957 and died in space.

A SPACE <u>HERO</u> SPEAKS

"We shouldn't have done it ... We did not learn enough from this mission to justify the death of the dog."
Soviet space-scientist Oleg Gazenko speaks about the death of Laika.

Want to know more about the most famous space-dog ever? Turn to page 28!

SPACED OUT!

Animals have been going into space since the 1940s. The very first were some fruit flies on a US rocket in 1947. They survived but not all the animals were as fortunate:

- In 1948, a monkey called Albert **suffocated** on board his spacecraft. Another monkey, Albert II, died in a crash landing the following year.

- During the early 1950s, US scientists mainly sent mice into space. Later in the decade, they began to use monkeys once again. The USSR (Union of Soviet Socialist Republics) launched 57 flights carrying dogs, with some intrepid hounds going into space more than once.

- By the 1960s, mice, rats, fruit flies, rabbits, plants, chimpanzees, frogs, wasps, beetles, a tortoise, and a French cat called Félicette had all made it into space. (It was only in 1961 that the **cosmonaut** Yuri Gagarin became the first human in space.)

▲ Ham, the first chimpanzee in space.

▲ Arabella, one of two spiders on board the Skylab space station. Amazingly, they quickly learned how to spin neat webs in Zero-G conditions.

No, it's an experiment!

Doing the spacewalk

It's time for a spacewalk! You know how in the movies, someone on a spacewalk comes loose from their craft and goes sailing off into space, never to be seen again? Well, don't worry. That's NEVER happened in real life. Well, not yet – so pay attention!

Suiting up

You need to put on your spacesuit hours before the spacewalk. Once sealed in, you'll breathe pure oxygen, which flushes all the nitrogen out of your blood. This is very important, as nitrogen can form bubbles and this can cause tremendous pain, brain injuries, or even death.

Remind yourself how spacesuits work by whizzing back to page 9!

Through the airlock

You leave the spacestation through an airlock, a system of two doors with a small chamber in-between. Both doors have an airtight seal: go out through one, close it, then open the other and climb out into space. (Don't forget to close the doors, or all the air will be sucked out of the space station and you'll be in a lot of trouble.)

▼ Astronauts during the construction of the International Space Station.

BLAST FROM THE PAST

In 1965, Alexei Leonov became the first spacewalker. He spent ten minutes outside, after which his suit had malfunctioned and blown up like a balloon. It wouldn't fit back into the spacecraft, so he had to let some oxygen out to avoid being stuck out in space.

Safety in space

During a spacewalk, astronauts are kept safe in a variety of ways ...

SECRET LINGO

Remember not to call it a 'spacewalk'. Its proper name is 'extra-vehicular activity' but everyone just calls it an 'EVA'.

▲ A robot arm helps the astronaut move around (and holds on to them). The grip is 100 times stronger than a human's. The extra-tough spacesuit is designed to protect the astronaut from mini-meteors.

▲ A tether (like a strong rope) makes sure the astronaut cannot drift away from the space station. Tools are also tethered to the astronaut.

▲ A jetpack backpack has 24 small thrusters, which squirt out jets of gas to move the astronaut around.

Touchdown!

When your time on the space station is up (or if they find out you're a bluffer and send you home early), it's time to return to Earth. Pay attention: the return to the planet's surface is probably the most dangerous part of your entire mission.

All aboard!

The *Soyuz TMA-M* descent module that astronauts use to get back to Earth only carries three people: it's a tight fit. The crew members climb in through the hatch and take their seats. The hatch is closed and the capsule undocks from the space station.

▲ The *Soyuz TMA-08M* spacecraft departs from the International Space Station.

Back into the atmosphere

Next comes a period of 'free flight', circling the Earth until the right spot for re-entry is reached. This is crucial: unless the capsule enters the atmosphere at the correct place, you will find yourself landing somewhere unexpected. Fortunately, the *Soyuz* is fitted with rockets that allow the flight commander to manoeuvre it.

▲ Seen from the International Space Station, the *Soyuz TMA-05M* descent module begins to re-enter the Earth's atmosphere.

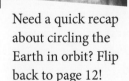

Need a quick recap about circling the Earth in orbit? Flip back to page 12!

Get the angle right

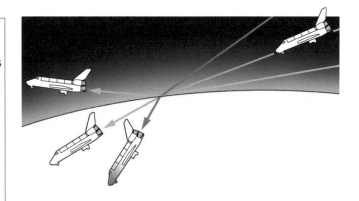

Key
- Angle too shallow? The capsule bounces off the atmosphere, back into space.
- Angle correct! The crew is protected by the heat shield.
- Angle too steep? The capsule gets too hot and fries to a crisp.

A red-hot ride

The speed of descent causes the outside of the descent module to glow red-hot so you'll be pleased to know the capsule is fitted with special heat shields. As you approach the Earth's surface, the parachutes are opened and rockets fire to cushion the landing even more. You still land with quite a bump though!

▲ The *Soyuz TMA-04M* spacecraft is seen as it lands in a remote area of Kazakhstan.

BLAST FROM THE PAST

Astronauts used to find it difficult to stand up when they got back to Earth and kept falling over. This was because in the Zero-G of space, their muscles hadn't been fighting gravity: they got so weak that they didn't really work any more. To avoid this, today's astronauts spend several hours a day exercising.

A SPACE HERO SPEAKS

"Any landing you can walk away from is a good one."
Astronaut Alan Shepard

Space greats

Hopefully, you've learnt enough now to successfully bluff your way into space and back again. Who knows, maybe one day you might even take your place amongst the space greats.

MOST FAMOUS SPACE ANIMAL

Name: Laika
Nationality: Russian
Claim to fame: Before she went into space, Laika, which is Russian for 'barker', was a stray dog on the streets of Moscow, Russia. She was trained to be the first animal in orbit. It was a prize no one would have wanted: Laika's Sputnik capsule was not designed to return to Earth and she died in space on 3rd November 1957.

FIRST WOMAN IN SPACE

Name: Valentina Tereshkova
Nationality: Russian
Claim to fame: In June 1963, at the age of just 26, Valentina Tereshkova became the first woman in space. She spent three days in orbit. It was an amazing achievement, especially for someone who not long before had been working in a cotton mill.

FIRST HUMAN ON THE MOON

Name: Neil Armstrong
Nationality: American

Claim to fame: In the early 1960s, the USSR was far ahead of the USA in space exploration. The US decided that to catch up, it would have to send a mission to the Moon. In 1969, Neil Armstrong, Buzz Aldrin and Michael Collins blasted off. Armstrong and Aldrin landed on the surface of the Moon, and Armstrong, the mission commander, was first out of the landing module.

HEROIC MISSION COMMANDER

Name: Jim Lovell
Nationality: American

Claim to fame: Lovell is one of only three people who have flown to the Moon twice. It was his second mission, Apollo 13, that made Lovell famous. Two days after launch, an oxygen tank exploded. The spacecraft lost power: it became extremely cold, there was no drinking water and the air inside was poisoned by carbon monoxide fumes. Despite this, four days after the explosion, *Apollo 13* returned safely to Earth.

So, can you bluff your way into space?

Try bluffing your way through this space quiz to find out if you could bluff your way into space one day …

1 Where does space start?

A: 80.5 kilometres high
B: 100 kilometres up
C: Above the highest clouds

2 What is Russian cosmonaut Pavel Vinogradov famous for?

A: Being former commander of the International Space Station
B: Making seven spacewalks
C: Being the first person to pay his **income tax** from space

3 What's the largest animal sent into space?

A: A small crocodile
B: A chimp
C: A dog

4 What does LEO mean?

A: Lovely Earth Orbit
B: Little Earth Orbit
C: Low Earth Orbit

5 How fast do you have to go to escape Earth's gravity?

A: 40 320 kph
B: It depends how heavy your spacecraft is
C: Ten times as fast as a Formula One car

6 How fast do you have to go to get back INTO Earth's atmosphere?

A: The same speed as when you leave
B: Slower than when you leave
C: Faster than when you leave

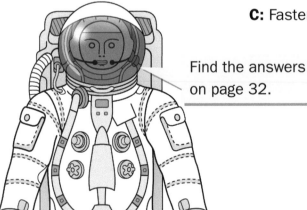

Find the answers on page 32.

Glossary

4-G	four times the gravitational force felt on Earth
buff	a person who is interested in and knows a lot about a particular subject
comfort break	to go to the toilet
cosmonaut	Russian term for astronaut
centrifuge	a machine with a rapidly rotates a container
dense	tightly packed
dock	to connect to (the opposite is **undock**)
escape velocity	The speed that allows a spacecraft to break free of Earth's gravity
glare	bright light
income tax	money you have to pay to the government based on how much you earn
jettison	to cast off or abandon
Low Earth Orbit	is an orbit between 160 km and 2000 km above Earth
nose cone	the pointed nose of a rocket-powered launch vehicle
payload	material carried by a spacecraft, such as cargo, equipment, passengers and satellites
quarantine	isolation intended to stop the spread of disease
radiation	harmful particles given off by some substances, such as uranium and plutonium
retract	to take back or withdraw.
shut-eye	a slang word for sleep
Snoopy	a dog character in a famous US cartoon strip
space sickness	also known as 'space adaptation syndrome', space sickness is similar to travel sickness
spacesuit	an outfit worn by astronauts while in space. There are different kinds for various activities, including lift-off and landing, and spacewalks.
suffocated	die because you do not have enough air to breathe
telemetry	the collection of data by a computer; the data is then beamed back to a control centre to be analysed.

Index

Answers

1: B (or A if you're American) – The Fédération Aéronautique Internationale, the international governing body for such matters, says space begins 100 km up. The USA says space starts at 80.5 km.

2: All three, but mainly the taxes.

3: A chimp – several chimps have been to space, the first being Ham, in 1961. Ham had been trained to pull levers aboard his spacecraft, which proved that movement was possible during take-off.

4: C – although everyone says it's lovely up there as well.

5: A – which translates as 672 km a minute, or 11.2 km a second. The fastest a Formula One car has ever gone is 413 kph.

6: C.